Original title:
The Merman's Lullaby

Copyright © 2025 Creative Arts Management OÜ
All rights reserved.

Author: Lucas Harrington
ISBN HARDBACK: 978-1-80587-257-3
ISBN PAPERBACK: 978-1-80587-727-1

Stars Above the Sea's Silent Depths

In waters deep where giggles flow,
A fishy prince puts on a show.
He sings to crabs and turtles bright,
With bubbles popping, what a sight!

His harp made of a broken shell,
He strums out tunes, oh what a swell!
The seahorses join in a dance,
While silly clams begin to prance.

With jellyfish that softly glow,
They twirl around in a wobbly row.
The starfish clap with tiny hands,
As laughter echoes through the sands.

Oh listen close, the ocean hums,
While seaweed plays on rubber drums.
A chorus of the loudest cheer,
The funny fish are gathered here!

Melodious Mists and Floating Fantasies

In misty waves where shadows tease,
A turtle juggles jelly peas.
The octopus, with eight long arms,
Plays peek-a-boo, and laughs in charms.

A dolphin hops with grace so sly,
And winks at seagulls passing by.
With bubbles rising, they all squeak,
As sea otters play hide and seek.

A chorus of the underwater crew,
With snappy snaps of clam's "I do!"
A lobster wears a crown so grand,
While dancing crabs dissolve the sand.

The merfolk giggle on their rafts,
As fish are telling silly drafts.
Oh float along in fancy dreams,
As laughter bubbles with the streams!

Bedtime in the Brine

In the depths where fish do snore,
Crabs do dance on the ocean floor.
Starfish twirl in the moonlight glow,
A sleepy wave says it's time to go.

Mermaids giggle, tangled in hair,
Seahorses ride without a care.
Jellyfish jiggle, glow with delight,
While clams clap shells, 'Goodnight, goodnight!'

Aisle of Seafoam Shadows

In shadows made of seafoam bright,
Fish wear pajamas, oh what a sight!
Octopus reads tales of sunken ships,
While shrimp sip tea with fancy flips.

Waves tickle toes as they pass by,
Gulls join in with a raucous cry.
Dolphins make waves as they dash around,
And sea turtles snooze on the ocean's mound.

Moonlit Melody of the Abyss

The moon hangs low, casting a tune,
Crabs play drums, who needs a spoon?
Eels do the cha-cha, tails in a twist,
While clams throw shells to join the list.

A conch shell horn calls out with cheer,
Echoing laughter for all to hear.
Fiddler fish strum with glee,
And starfish clap, 'Oh, sing with me!'

Sheltered by Seaweed Dreams

Beneath a blanket of seaweed green,
Fish dream of places they've never seen.
Giggling bubbles tickle their toes,
As sea turtles drift in sleepy doze.

The depths hold secrets of sandy shores,
While crabs tell jokes of legendary roars.
Giant squids keep time with their ink,
In a world where fish dance, seldom do they think.

Treasure of Tranquil Tides

In the deep where bubbles gleam,
Silly fish dance and beam.
A crab sings loud, a clam joins in,
While seaweed sways, it's quite a din.

Octopus twirls, a silly sight,
With eight arms waving, oh what a fright!
Starfish giggles, lost in the fun,
Who needs rest when the party's begun?

A treasure chest filled with jellybeans,
The silliest catch in the fishy scenes.
Mermaids laugh, they flip and glide,
In the treasure of tranquil tides.

Beneath the Surface Lull

Down below where fish all huddle,
Turtles giggle in a bubble.
Shark tries to dance, what a clumsy feat,
Who knew fins could be so discreet?

Dolphins prank with a leap and splash,
Jellyfish float, oh what a clash!
Under the waves, silliness reigns,
Beneath the surface, joy remains.

Seashells echo a tickling jest,
Giggling waves never let them rest.
Crabs tell tales of shoes and socks,
In their underwater paradox.

Ocean's Whispering Cradle

In a cradle of nights so blue,
Whales hum tunes; they joke, it's true.
Seahorses race on bubble bikes,
Each twist and turn, full of spikes.

With a wink, the plankton glow,
Making sea sprites put on a show.
Anemones dance in funny jigs,
While clams bring snacks, those bouncy digs.

Stars twinkle down on the watery play,
Fish crack jokes at the end of day.
In this cradle, laughter's a wave,
Ocean's whispers, playful and brave.

Deep Blue Melodies

In the sea, the fish do dance,
Wearing hats and pants by chance.
Crabs play tunes on seashell drums,
While dolphins wiggle to the hums.

Starfish strut in snazzy gear,
Jellyfish giggle, nothing to fear.
Turtles join the jolly choir,
Their voices lifting ever higher!

Tides of Enchanted Slumber

Bubbles float like dreams in night,
Sleepy whales snore with delight.
Octopuses knit with delight,
Stitching seaweed blankets tight.

Sea horses spin in sleepy grace,
Trying to keep up the pace.
All around the coral beds,
Fish bubble breezy sleepy threads.

Sirens' Soft Embrace

Mermaids hum with cheeky glee,
Tickling fish down by the sea.
Their laughter spills like waves of cheer,
Echoing far, both bright and clear.

With seashells trumpeting their charm,
They pull you close without a harm.
Even crabs join in the fun,
Wiggling 'til the day is done!

Aquatic Harmony at Dusk

At twilight, fish play cosmic games,
Creating ripples, casting names.
Turtles toss their sleepy heads,
As seaweed cradles all their beds.

Whales whirl in a sleepy trance,
Swaying softly, caught in chance.
Fishy friends all gather 'round,
In this watery playground found.

Lost in the Undertow of Dreams

In a bubble of seaweed, I float with glee,
Chasing fish that giggle, oh what a spree!
Octopus tickles, my toes and my nose,
Crabs wear glasses, in wacky repose.

Mermaids dance with sea turtles in tow,
Their hair made of shells, they put on a show!
A shark comes by, with a goofy grin,
Says, 'Join the fun, let the dreaming begin!'

Ebb and Flow of Slumber

Waves crash softly like pillows at night,
Starfish whisper secrets, oh what a sight!
Dolphins laugh at the moon's silly beam,
While jellyfish float in a whimsical dream.

Clams clap their shells to a sea song so bright,
As crabs do the cha-cha, what a delight!
With a splash and a wink, they invite me near,
To snooze in the tide, where no worries appear.

Sheltered by Sea Mist

Wrapped in sea mist, far from the tide,
A turtle named Tum-Tum hops by my side.
With a wink of his eye and a flip of his tail,
He tells me of fish that love to set sail.

They giggle and splash, play tag with the foam,
In this underwater world, I feel at home.
A pirate fish grins with a treasure chest,
Says, 'Join my crew, you'll surely be blessed!'

Kaleidoscope of Quiet Currents

In a world of colors, the sea swirls around,
With rainbow fish flipping, oh what a sound!
A clam wearing shoes does a jitterbug dance,
While sea stars twinkle, they love a good chance.

Seahorses giggle with bubbles of cheer,
As I hold my breath, feeling no fear.
Each wave a tickle, each tide a new game,
In the depths of my dreams, nothing's the same!

Seafoam Whispers of Nightfall

In the depths, where seaweed sways,
A fish wears sunglasses, soaking rays.
Bubbles giggle, making sound,
As crabs do the jig upon the ground.

Seahorses dance, while mermaids sing,
Shells gossip 'bout a treasure fling.
With every splash, the octopus grins,
As starfish ponder their next win.

Underwater Reverie

Beneath the waves, the conch shells chat,
A dolphin's joke? It's so old, it's flat.
Pufferfish puff for a glow-up spree,
While clownfish laugh, as funny as can be.

The jellyfish float, a wobbly sight,
With each wibble, they twinkle with light.
And here comes a crab, with a dance so fine,
Saying, 'Hey, wave! I'm the life of the line!'

Tranquility Beneath the Surface

Turtles talk of the best laid plans,
While sea cucumbers chill in their bands.
A whale named Bob tells tales so grand,
Of bumper cars made of driftwood and sand.

As currents swirl, the fish joke around,
While turtles grin, so wisdom-bound.
The sea breeze chuckles with each passing wave,
Beneath the calm, it's a wild rave!

Cry of the Whales

In the deep, where songs do play,
Whales belt out tunes in the silliest way.
A sea lion's laugh echoes like cheer,
As plankton party with nibbles of beer.

'Why did the fish cross the ocean wide?'
To show off its glitter and swim with pride!
With bubbles galore and laughter so bright,
The ocean's a stage, a comical sight!

Gentle Waves

Waves roll in with a gentle giggle,
Sand crabs shuffle, and seahorses wiggle.
With shells as hats, they parade the shore,
Jellyfish wagging, asking for more!

The laughter spreads like ripples do,
As fish play hide-n-seek with a view.
A funny fish tells a tale of a cat,
The ocean grins, where silliness sat!

Twilight Tides and the Ocean's Peace

Bubbles pop with giggles bright,
Seaweed dances, what a sight!
Fishies swirl in silly plays,
At dusk, they laugh in watery ways.

Turtles chase a jelly's glow,
Swapping tales from down below.
Crabs in hats sing off-key songs,
While dolphins flip, it's where fun belongs.

Starfish throw confetti shells,
Clownfish ringing tiny bells.
The ocean sparkles, smiles grin wide,
A party in the shifting tide.

Drowsy Echoes of Deep Waters

In the depths where laughter flows,
Octopus juggling, everyone knows!
With tiny claps, the minnows cheer,
As sleepy waves sway, bringing cheer.

Seahorse slides on slippery trails,
Creating bubbles, silly tales.
The anglerfish, a shining star,
Winks at shrimp from afar.

Napping whales hum a tune,
Snoring soft beneath the moon.
As currents swirl, they softly snore,
While fish gather, wanting more.

Drift Away with Aquatic Dreams

Here in blue where laughter gleams,
Dreams take flight on jolly beams.
Sandy mermaids start to twirl,
With conch-shell phones to give a whirl.

Tadpoles twang their makeshift strings,
Crooner frogs sharing comedy flings.
A splash of color, scales of gold,
Chasing jellies, stories unfold.

As playful waves lap at the shore,
Mollusks giggle, always wanting more.
A sleepy tide hums lullabies,
With every splash, the humor flies.

Soft Waves and Submerged Whispers

Much like secrets, waters hum,
Mariners giggle, drumming drums.
With every ripple, laughter grows,
Whispers echo where sea grass blows.

Fish in bow ties twirl around,
Shells keep the rhythm, sounds abound.
Anemones tickle with playful glee,
A sanctuary of winks and spree.

Waves may crash, but who cares?
Seals juggle shells without any snares.
As moonlight glimmers, joy's the key,
In depths of water, it's all carefree.

Abyssal Dreams in Sapphire Depths

In bubbles, fishy giggles play,
As finned friends wiggle, dance away.
A kraken's smile, a whale's own grin,
In ocean depths, their fun begins.

They splash and twirl in salty waves,
Tickling toes of sinking knaves.
With seaweed hats and jelly tails,
They throw wild parties, tell some tales.

A clam sings out a silly tune,
While octopuses groove by moon.
They dunk and dive, a comical site,
In depths where laughter feels so right.

So close your eyes, feel ocean's sway,
In dreams where fishes frolic and play.
With laughter echoing through your sleep,
These watery joys, forever keep.

Siren's Moonlit Song

Beneath the stars, a siren's call,
With wobbly notes, she charms us all.
Her voice, a mix of squeaks and squawks,
Creates a dance in ocean docks.

Her fishy friends flip-flop about,
Each gurgling laugh, a joyful shout.
They twirl and spin like silly beasts,
In salty lanes, they throw great feasts.

But watch your step, don't lose your way,
As sea cucumbers start to play.
With slippery moves and silly spins,
They pull you in for ocean wins.

So hitch a ride on frothy surf,
Join all the fun, and let it swerve.
With moonlit joy in briny air,
You'll giggle with the creatures rare.

Indigos and Dreamscapes

In the depths of blue, dreams collide,
Where sea snails dance and eels abide.
A bubble train rides by so fast,
With sea horses pulling, such a blast!

Their laughter rings through swirling tides,
In whimsical worlds where fun resides.
With starfish claps and crabby cheers,
They celebrate through endless years.

Jellyfish float on giggling streams,
While tiny shrimps share silly dreams.
Through corals bright, they prank and tease,
Creating chuckles in ocean breeze.

So close your eyes, dive deep and wide,
In this silly world, come take a ride.
With depths so bright and giggles sweet,
Your heart will dance to the ocean's beat.

Starlit Waters Luring You Home

At twilight's wink, the waters glow,
With tales of fish and squeaky foes.
A playful dolphin shows his dance,
While creatures join in for a prance.

The bubbles float with giggling sounds,
As sea turtles spin in frothy rounds.
With clams a-clapping and starfish swaying,
This underwater ball is worth delaying.

The seaweeds sway, a green ballet,
As crabs compete in their weird way.
With slippery slips and splashy sparks,
They host a show that surely marks.

So if you hear a funny song,
In starlit waves where you belong,
Jump in the fun, forget the strife,
In this wet world, you'll find your life.

Lull of the Aquatic Night

In waters deep, where fish swim by,
A seahorse sings, oh my, oh my!
With bubbles burst, and frothy cheer,
Crabs join in, let's all draw near.

The octopus plays a jazzy beat,
While starfish dance with happy feet.
The clownfish jokes, it's quite a sight,
As bedtime comes, a silly night.

The jellyfish glow, like disco balls,
While turtles roll and giggle in halls.
With every wave, the laughter swells,
In ocean's arms, where joy compels.

So close your eyes, and dream of fun,
In the sea where we all run.
A lull of bubbles, bright and light,
Let your dreams take playful flight.

Pearls and Echoes of Slumber

In a bay where sea birds hoot,
Lies a turtle with a fruit suit.
He tells of pearls that wiggle round,
As laughter bubbles up from the ground.

The dolphin flips, the lobster claps,
While playful seaweed gently naps.
Anemones sway, all tickled pink,
As fish join in, they giggle and wink.

With whispers soft, the waves bring cheer,
While crabs prepare a feast, oh dear!
They serve up snacks, in fancy style,
With jelly spread that makes you smile.

So rest your head, let the sea hum low,
In dreams of pearls, let laughter flow.
As echoes play in the watery night,
You'll wake to joy, feeling just right.

Dusky Waters and Whispered Wishes

In dusky waters, shadows play,
A fish with glasses shouts, 'Hooray!'
With whispers dreaming of tasty treats,
The swell of laughter never retreats.

A crab with style wears a top hat,
While jellyfish glide, looking quite fat.
They dance and sway in the twilight glow,
As all the critters put on a show.

The waves call out, a serenade,
While snails spin tales, their friends invade.
A fish on a scooter, what a sight,
Spreading giggles in the marine light.

So hug your shells, and close those eyes,
While starlit fish dive and rise.
With wishes whispered, laughter blooms,
Adventure awaits in watery rooms.

Hush of the Deep Blue Night

In the hush of night, where fishes dream,
A grouper croons with a silvery gleam.
The angelfish giggle, the waves applaud,
As sea creatures join in the nighttime facade.

A clam with a grin lends a playful tune,
While sea turtles nap beneath the moon.
The narwhal spins in a dizzy dance,
While fishes float in a dreamy trance.

Oh, bubbles rise, with whispering fun,
A sea urchin shares jokes with everyone.
As laughter echoes through coral halls,
The ocean's embrace gently calls.

So drift away where the mermaids play,
With goofy dreams in a salty sway.
The hush of night will guard your sleep,
In waters where jovial secrets keep.

Siren's Slumber Song

Bubbles float and fish are snoring,
Crabs are dreaming, waves are soaring.
A seaweed blanket wraps around,
With giggles here, and snores abound.

Starfish yawn in silly forms,
Jellyfish dance in dreamlike swarms.
Octopuses tuck in their arms tight,
As sea turtles wink at the moonlight.

Dolphins chuckle, rolling on waves,
Counting clams and bearded knaves.
Seahorses whisper secret tales,
Of treasure hunts and wind-filled sails.

Sleep tight, my friends, the tide may tease,
But drift away with the gentle breeze.
In this watery world, laughter rings,
As dreams afloat on salty wings.

Tranquil Tides and Sleepy Sands

Down beneath the sandy shore,
Crabs wear pajamas, what a roar!
Seagulls giggle, one took a dive,
While fish play tag, oh how they thrive!

Anemones sway in bubble beds,
While sea urchins rest their silly heads.
With shells for pillows, oceans hum,
As sleepy sea creatures softly drum.

Whales tell jokes in lower tones,
Echoing laughter in rolling moans.
Shrimps wear hats made of bright coral,
Having a ball, oh, what a moral!

Sleepy tides swirl in funny dreams,
As flounders slide on moonlit beams.
In sandcastles of wobbly grace,
Every creature finds its cozy place.

Melodies of Frosted Fins

Frosty fins in winter's glow,
Sea otters float with cheeks aglow.
They sing a tune of snowy cheer,
As sea cucumbers clap and cheer.

Fish in scarves swim by with flair,
Jokes in bubbles float through the air.
Coral reefs wear winter hats,
While krill ballet with crafty spats.

An icy squid makes funny faces,
While dolphins race through crystal spaces.
Suspended laughter in chilly waves,
As frozen seas hide giggling knaves.

So rest your eyes in frosty delight,
With whiskered friends on a starry night.
In watery dreams, let laughter spin,
With melodies of frosted fins.

Starfish Lullabies and Ocean Breezes

Starfish wink with sleepy eyes,
As gentle waves hum lullabies.
Octopus twirls in soft moonlight,
Crab shuffles home, a silly sight.

Seahorses whisper secrets low,
To sleepy clams, while tides ebb slow.
A whale's sonnet, a splashy scene,
Puffers puff in between the gleam.

Sand dollars dance, a quirky crew,
As pufferfish giggle, 'What's new?'
Mermaids weave tales of playful pranks,
While slippery eels perform on banks.

The ocean sighs, a sleepy breeze,
Blowing dreams through tangled seas.
In this world where laughter spins,
Close your eyes, let the joy begin.

Calming Rhythms of the Deep

Bubbles rise and giggles glide,
Fishy friends come out to hide.
Sea cucumbers dance with flair,
While an octopus combs its hair.

Crabs in pajamas, what a sight,
Throwing shells in the moonlight.
They waltz with the currents, a balmy breeze,
Enjoying seaweed snacks with glee!

Tides tap-dance, waves like drums,
Seahorses hum as the twilight comes.
Mermaids chuckle, tickle their toes,
As jellyfish sway in soft pink glow.

Snoozing whales make a grand show,
Spouting water, and off they go.
In dreams of seaweed, laughter blooms,
Beneath the waves, where fun resumes.

Nautical Naptime Melodies

Barnacles sing in a sleepy tune,
Sailing clouds under a silver moon.
Dolphins giggle, splashing about,
Tickling each other and laughing out loud.

Crustaceans napping on sandy beds,
With tiny pillows and sleepy heads.
Starfish in pajamas, all tucked in tight,
Counting bubbles to dreamland tonight.

Sardines swirl in a dance so sweet,
While clams snore softly, oh what a treat!
Seashells whisper, "Just close your eyes,"
As seaweed sways under starlit skies.

Gulls serenade with a squawking cheer,
"Don't you fret, dear, we're all right here!"
With laughter echoing through the bay,
In this dreamy world, we play and play.

Whispers from the Depths of the Sea

Flippered whispers, tales of old,
Mermaids chuckling in waters cold.
Shrimps spilling secrets with each bright snap,
As pillowfish snooze in their cozy lap.

Bubbles float by with giggling sounds,
A turtled parade, where joy abounds.
Clownfish tease with a playful flip,
While sea stars pose for a sleepy dip.

The anchor's dropped, let's take a rest,
In a coral cradle, we're surely blessed.
With crabby lullabies and jellyfish lights,
The ocean croons sweet through the nights.

Seashells snuggle with wishes and dreams,
As jolly sea turtles drift in streams.
In the soft tides of a watery spree,
Laughter lingers, wild and free.

Cradled by Currents

The waves are rocking, a gentle tide,
Where playful sea otters slip and slide.
Caught in a whirl of tickles and cheer,
They roll and tumble, spreading good cheer.

Anemones dance, wearing flower crowns,
While fishes giggle in their underwater towns.
A seagull shouts, "Hey, don't make a mess!"
As bubbles burst with a watery press.

Starfish give hugs, all soft and bright,
And sea turtles share stories through the night.
With coral castles glowing and gleam,
We drift in laughter, lost in a dream.

So close your eyes, let the tides take hold,
With ocean songs, as the night unfolds.
Cradled by currents, we find our way,
In this watery world, where we laugh and play.

The Harmony of Drowned Stars

Bubbles rise with silly sounds,
Fishy giggles all around.
Starfish dance in wobbly glee,
Swaying gently by the sea.

Drifting tides with a funny tune,
Octopus jigs under the moon.
Seahorses prance in a wacky line,
All laugh as they sip on brine.

Crabs with swords in playful duels,
Chasing clams, those crafty fools.
Mermaids chuckle, twinkling hair,
As they toss seaweed everywhere.

A conch shell whispers goofy dreams,
Of sea turtle ice cream schemes.
The deep blue echoes with silly cheer,
As starry fish swim without a fear.

Sleep Under the Seafoam

Wavelets play with silvery hugs,
Tickling toes of sleepy shrugs.
Crabs find cozy little beds,
While starfish rest their tiny heads.

Dolphins yawn in swirling spins,
Giggling softly, making fins.
Seashells snore in rhythmic sighs,
Echoed gently with fishy cries.

Plankton twirl in bedtime jest,
As sleepy sharks take their best.
The ocean hums a lull, then grins,
With bubbles popping where it begins.

Mermaids weave a dreamer's net,
Catching laughs they won't forget.
In seafoam beds of frothy white,
The ocean laughs into the night.

Nightfall in the Coral Kingdom

Coral castles dressed in glee,
A jellyfish floats with a cup of tea.
Seahorses giggle on a merry-go-round,
Celebrating joy that knows no bound.

The clams sing sweet in a boisterous key,
While crabs pull pranks as light as a flea.
In nocturnal fun, the fish play tag,
Under the moon, no room for a lag.

Starry fish with hats so bright,
Making jokes 'til the morning light.
Even the seaweed sways with flair,
Dancing lightly without a care.

So close your eyes in ocean deep,
And dream of laughter as you sleep.
With every wave a giggle near,
The Coral Kingdom's joy is clear.

Waves Crashing in Reverie

Waves roll in with a bubbly splash,
Tickling toes in a merry dash.
Surfers ride on giggles' crest,
As dolphins lead the frothy jest.

Seagulls squawk with laugh-filled cries,
While clam shanties reach for the skies.
A fish in a top hat makes a scene,
Juggling seashells, oh so keen!

Starfish giggle at their beachy friends,
As painted squids make art that bends.
Jellybeans float in vibrant hues,
A candy feast from salty blues.

So let the surf sing sweet and bright,
As laughter echoes through the night.
With every wave, a smile you'll find,
In this dreamy, quirky ocean grind.

Nightfall in the Coral Garden

Bubbles dance as seaweed sways,
Fish in pajamas start their plays.
Octopus juggles shells with flair,
Clownfish giggle, no worries, no care.

Moonlight glints on waves that tease,
Starfish yoga brings the ocean ease.
A crab in a tutu prances around,
While sea turtles spin, they've lost all ground.

Whispering Shells and Midnight Light

Shells confide their secrets bold,
Gossiping tales of treasures untold.
A dolphin sings in a goofy tone,
While wrasses chuckle, never alone.

Glowfish twinkle like stars in the sea,
Flipping their fins with mischievous glee.
A seahorse with glasses carefully reads,
Comics of krill, what a funny breed!

Hidden Harmonies of the Deep

Anemones sway, they're quite the sight,
Playing hide and seek with the fading light.
A grouchy grouper sings off-key,
While plankton giggle and dance with glee.

Squids in a band, drumming on rocks,
While lobsters mimic their itchy socks.
Harmony's chaos under the spell,
As the ocean broadcasts its comedic swell.

Shadows Beneath the Silver Surface

Turtles chase shadows, they sight a snack,
A dinner of jelly that they'll never unpack.
Chasing their tails, what a silly sight,
Bantering banjo fish add to the night.

Sea cucumbers laugh, wiggling slow,
While beneath them, a clam steals the show.
With flippers a-floppin', the party's a blast,
In the depths of the ocean, the fun's unsurpassed.

Swaying Seaweed Serenade

In waters deep where seaweed sways,
The fish have dances in a merry maze.
With giggles and bubbles, they twist and twirl,
An underwater party with an oceanic whirl.

Octopus juggling shells with flair,
Clownfish laughing, they float on air.
A crab on the conga, what a sight to see,
While starfish clap in total glee.

A dolphin joins in with a funny flip,
Splashing seafoam on a tiny shrimp.
As laughter echoes through the salty spray,
The ocean's a stage, come join the play!

So if you feel blue, just dive right in,
Join the goofy sea crew, let the fun begin!
With notes of seaweed in vibrant hues,
You'll leave with a smile, and maybe some blue shoes.

Rest Beneath the Waves

Beneath the waves, where critters nap,
The snoring seals create a flap.
A turtle spins on a cozy bed,
While fish tiptoe softly, avoiding the dread.

Anemones chuckle in soothing tides,
Seahorses whisper with giggling grins wide.
While crabs doze off in their sandy shrouds,
The ocean rocks gently, soothing the crowds.

When shrimp start to tap dance, it's time to wake,
A squirrelfish sneezes, oh what a mistake!
The laughter erupts as all come alive,
With sloshing and splashes, they giggle and dive.

Just rest and relax in this watery frame,
Where everyone's silly, and nothing's the same.
In this whimsical world beneath the foam,
You'll find fun in the currents—call it home!

Dreams Drifting with the Currents

Dreams drift along with the playful tide,
Where jellyfish float and nowhere to hide.
A fish with a hat swims by with grace,
While eels play tag in their slippery race.

A narwhal hums a tuneful song,
While mermaids giggle, they can't help but throng.
The sea turtles roll, carefree and wild,
Chasing the bubbles, like a silly child.

Under the moonlight, secrets are shared,
With laughter that echoes, no one is scared.
As laughter fills the salty air,
The ocean hosts dreams, all merry and rare.

So let your heart drift with the tide today,
Join the underwater fun in your own quirky way.
With waves of chuckles and currents of play,
You'll find delight in the depths of the bay!

Chorus of the Echoing Depths

In the depths below where the echoes sing,
A chorus of fish brings joy in a fling.
With wrasses in tuxedos and gobies in hats,
They groove through the water with rhythm and spats.

A salmon starts crooning a silly old tune,
While pufferfish giggle and bounce like a balloon.
The squid are the dancers, with moves so slick,
Spinning and swirling, a graceful flick.

With bubbles as notes, and waves as the beat,
The ocean's alive with a festival sweet.
A clownfish takes center stage with a roar,
As sea turtles clap, demanding encore.

So tune in your fins and let out a cheer,
In the chorus of depths, laughter's sincere.
For beneath the blue, in this cosmic ballet,
The sea holds a party: come join the display!

Lull of the Luminous Shores

In waters bright with gleaming fish,
A crab named Fred has one big wish.
He dreams of dancing on the sand,
But first, he needs a helping hand.

The seagulls laugh, they flap and dive,
While Fred's attempts keep him alive.
He twirls and spins, but slips and falls,
Yet giggles fill the ocean's halls.

A tide pool whispers, 'Join the fun!'
As seaweed sways, all day till done.
With every splash, the laughter grows,
This is the dance that everyone knows!

So join the party, seashells cheer,
With every wave, we bring good cheer.
For under stars, we shake and sway,
In luminous shores, we laugh and play!

Echoes of the Ocean's Heart

The dolphins giggle, they sound the call,
With flip and splash, they dance for all.
A whale nearby sings a big old song,
Everyone joins in, we can't go wrong!

The starfish twirl on sandy floors,
Wiggling limbs and silly roars.
With each wave that rolls on in,
Our ocean party will always win!

A jellyfish jives, glowing so bright,
In rhythms swaying, it feels just right.
While purple sea urchins roll and rock,
Together we laugh, we laugh 'til we drop!

Under the sun, with splashes galore,
From coral to kelp, we dance and explore.
So come dive deep, let worries fly,
With echoes of laughter beneath the sky!

Secrets Beneath the Sea

In a treasure chest, a clam named Lou,
Hides all the secrets, he thinks he knew.
But every time he goes to peek,
His friends pop out, and Lou lets out a squeak!

The octopus has eight long arms,
Each one playing silly charms.
With tickles here and splashes there,
Under the waves, joy fills the air!

A story told by a wise old crab,
Turns every frown into a fab!
For beneath the sea, what's funny and fun,
It's where the laughter's never done.

So dive down deep, where giggles grow,
With each new tale, we steal the show.
The secrets of the sea shall be,
Laughter and joy, our jubilee!

Celestial Waters and Gentle Breezes

The stars above look down and grin,
As water nymphs are bound to spin.
They throw a party on the moonlit waves,
Where mermaids leap and ocean raves!

With every splash, a giggle flies,
As sea turtles wear goofy ties.
A floating floaty, round and pink,
Bobs like a goose, we laugh and wink!

In celestial glow, we flaunt and jest,
A crab with shades thinks he's the best.
A clam joins in, clapping its shell,
We dance and twirl, all under the swell!

So gentle breezes whisper cheer,
In waters alive, we shed each fear.
For every wave, let laughter be,
In celestial waters, wild and free!

Balance of Waves and Wishes

In the ocean's dance, fish spin and twirl,
A conch shell sings while seaweed unfurl.
The starfish giggles, and crabs tap their feet,
Waves make a ruckus, oh, isn't that neat?

A dolphin dives deep with a splashy cheer,
While sea turtles chuckle, spreading good cheer.
The jellyfish float, in a luminous show,
In this silly splash party, they steal the show!

Seagulls squawk loudly, making quite a fuss,
The octopus juggles, oh, what a plus!
With each wave that rolls, dreams start to form,
A whimsical world, where all creatures swarm.

So let's join the fun, grab a seaweed hat,
And dance in the surf, with a splish and a splat!
In the balance of wishes, just let it unfold,
For laughter and joy stir the ocean's gold.

Nautical Notes of Rest

Underneath the stars, a fish choir sings,
While barnacles tap dance with shaky fins.
The waves hum a tune, soft and melodious,
With octopi harmonizing, oh so joyous!

Crabs form a band, with shells as their drums,
A sea snail plays flute, while everyone hums.
The seaweed sways gently, caught in the beat,
While sea horses waltz, in rhythm, so sweet.

As the moonlight glimmers on the water's face,
All sea creatures join in, a blissful embrace.
With laughter and bubbles that soar through the night,
This silly soiree is a pure delight!

And when dawn approaches, the giggles remain,
In the nautical notes, there's never a strain.
With dreams of tomorrow, in the ocean's warm thrall,
We drift off to sleep, hearing laughter's soft call.

Crystalline Calm of the Ocean's Heart

In the clear blue depths where the light prances,
Fish do ballet, taking their chances.
With smiles like rainbows and jokes to be told,
Their antics bright, never growing old.

The bubbles burst softly with giggles and cheers,
As crabs tell tall tales that tickle our ears.
A starfish winks, with a sly little grin,
As the dolphins swim by with a splash and a spin.

Coral reefs chuckle at every funny glance,
While sea cucumbers join in the dance.
With a wink and a nod, the waves come alive,
In this crystal-clear realm, where laughter will thrive.

So let the ocean tickle your funny bone,
With every wave's play, you'll never be alone.
In the crystalline calm, let your worries take flight,
For beneath the sea's surface, there's pure delight!

The Deep's Gentle Embrace

In the deep blue sea, where the odd fish play,
With seagrass hats making a whimsical array.
The squid pulls a prank, squirtin' ink with a laugh,
As sleepy fish gather for a goofy photograph!

A sleepy sea lion snoozes in peace,
While tiny shrimp giggle, their laughter won't cease.
In this underwater world, joy bubbles near,
As the sunbeams dance down, spreading warmth and cheer.

The turtles chatter, sharing tales of the past,
Their stories so silly, they hold us steadfast.
The deep's gentle embrace is a treasure of fun,
Where laughter unites us, and nobody's outdone.

So dive in the deep and let worries all fade,
With friends all around, in the games that we've played.
In the humor of tides, we find our own space,
Let's celebrate life with a splash and a grace!

Humming Tides of Tranquility

In the depths where fishy giggles sway,
A crab dances in a clumsy ballet.
Shells are huddled, gossiping shells,
Whispering tales of deep-sea swells.

The seaweed sways with a funky beat,
While dolphins shuffle their happy feet.
Starfish giggle, it's quite the scene,
In this underwater comedy routine.

Bubble talk echoes, as mermaids yawn,
Fins flapping softly at the break of dawn.
With laughter bubbling through coral homes,
They sing of ships and their mariner gnomes.

So rest your head on the ocean floor,
Where funny fish dance and squids encore.
Let the waves rock you like a lullaby,
In this humorous world, where giggles never die.

Night with a Soulful Salty Breeze

Beneath the stars that twinkle and tease,
Comes a whiff of chaos on the salty breeze.
A parrotfish sports a jazzy hat,
Cracking jokes while the octopus chats.

The tide rolls in, with a playful splash,
As seagulls waddle, ready to dash.
Crabs in bow ties, bringing their flair,
Funny fish tales fill the salty air.

Under the cover of shimmering light,
Urchins chuckle at all the sights.
Anemones sway to the rhythm so sweet,
While the flounders play tag with their webbed feet.

So gather round in this aquatic spree,
Where the sea sings softly, oh can't you see?
With giggles and gurgles, let's revel and soar,
In this funny night, who could ask for more?

Cradle of the Rolling Seas

Rocked by the waves of a bubbly view,
A dolphin plays peek-a-boo just for you.
Seashells giggle in harmonious fits,
While the starfish take breaks from their skits.

The kraken's got jokes, but they're somewhat shy,
Whispering laughter from the deep blue sky.
In the cradle of foamy waves so bright,
Aquatic critters dance till the night.

A clownfish grins with a wink of glee,
Telling tales of his deep-sea spree.
While turtles snicker at their age-old tales,
Of treasure hunts and stormy gales.

So sway with the current, let laughter leak,
For even the ocean has its cheeky streak.
In this cradle of giggles, afloat we'll remain,
Where humor flows like the salty rain.

Driftwood Dreams

On a raft of driftwood under silver stars,
Sardines play cards, sipping fizzy jars.
With laughter bubbling like the waves above,
The fish throw parties in the moonlight glove.

A wiggly worm with a top hat sings,
As the seaweed cowboys strum their strings.
In this underwater circus, oh so bright,
They spin and twirl in the soft moonlight.

Gull-fish perform with dramatic flair,
While jellyfish glow, floating in air.
The krill cheer on from the rocky shoals,
In this funny ballet of oceanic souls.

So dream sweet dreams on this salty tide,
With fishy comedians by your side.
In the driftwood realm, where silliness gleams,
Let the ocean cradle you in laughter-filled dreams.

Ocean's Lore

The waves curl up with a whimsy glow,
While the sea snails wiggle in a slapstick show.
The barnacles hoot with a whimsical cheer,
In the salty blue theater, nothing to fear.

Seahorses prance in polka-dot suits,
As lobsters gossip in funky boots.
They trade their secrets, each tale more absurd,
In this underwater realm, where jokes are heard.

With echoes of laughter in currents that flow,
The fish share wisdom from the ocean's slow.
A conch shell whispers of fun and delight,
In the tapestry woven of mirth every night.

So dive into stories from the depths evermore,
Where giggles and splashes create folklore.
In this realm of humor where warmth intertwines,
Ocean's lore sparkles like the sun that shines.

Undersea Sonatas and Moonlight

Bubbles rise in gleeful tones,
As fishy friends perform their drones.
Seaweed sways to the laughing breeze,
Crabs join in with clapping knees.

Octopuses juggle pearls so bright,
While turtles glide in dance of light.
Starfish twirl on the sandy floor,
As echoes of giggles fill the shore.

Seahorses prance with glittery flair,
Their party hats a rare sea wear.
Every wave sings a merry tune,
Under the watchful, chuckling moon.

Pitch a shell for the grand seashell choir,
With glee they sing, lift spirits higher.
Laughter bubbles, joy in each wave,
The ocean dances, it's quite the rave!

The Sleep that Dances with Fishes

Close your eyes, the tide will sway,
While guppies leap in a gamesome play.
Starry night over currents blue,
A waltz with a dolphin just for you.

The jellyfish float with jelly-like grace,
Waggling their tentacles, a funny face.
Clownfish giggle in playful delight,
As they chase bubbles in the pale moonlight.

A narwhal winks with its spiraled horn,
Cracking jokes as dawn is born.
Crabs scuttle while making a scene,
Rocking the seabed like a messy teen.

Sleep now, dear, in the ocean's embrace,
Where dreams are mixed in a fishy race.
With gentle snickers and waves of cheer,
Drift away, the sea's laughter near.

Dusk's Fluid Lullabies

As dusk creeps in with splashes of fun,
Fishes frolic; the play has begun!
Mermaids giggle with bubbles in tow,
While sea turtles dance in a slow, sly show.

A wise old whale hums a silly tune,
While jellies sway under the light of the moon.
With each flippered flap, the ocean sings,
And even the barnacles tap their rings.

Look! A seal with a shiny bow tie,
Leaps like a dancer, oh my, oh my!
Crabs take turns to tell a good joke,
While the seaweed shimmies in laughter's cloak.

So float on your dreams, let giggles cascade,
In this wavy world where friends are made.
A lullaby of laughter, sweet and spry,
Where even the fishy ones let out a sigh.

Gentle Currents of Peace

Gentle waves whisper tales untold,
Where sea creatures dance, brave and bold.
A grouchy old flounder finds a new groove,
And with wiggly fins, he starts to move.

Through kelp forests, laughter flows,
As anglerfish twinkle with goofy glows.
The snappy shrimp joins in the jest,
With a jump and a wiggle, he's at his best.

Gilly the shark plays peek-a-boo,
With maxed-out grins, a happy crew.
While soft breezes blow, and the sea hums low,
Nestled in currents, where laughter will grow.

So come join the fun in the brine and foam,
Each bubble a whisper of joy and home.
Rest in the waters where whimsy flows,
And let the ocean's chuckles be your prose.

Mysteries Cradled by the Current

In the deep where bubbles dance,
A fish with glasses sits by chance.
He reads a book of ancient lore,
While jellyfish knock at his door.

A crab in shoes struts down the sand,
Waving his claws, he feels quite grand.
A clam plays chess with a shy old whale,
As seaweed sways to a fishy tale.

Bubbles giggle, they drift and spin,
A dolphin laughs, says "Let's begin!"
They have a party, it's quite a sight,
With sea cucumbers dancing all night.

Oh, mysteries cradled by the tide,
Where sea critters smile, and joy can't hide.
From cranky otters to silly fluke,
In the murky depths, they begin to kook.

The Serene Song of Seashells

Singing shells on the sandy shore,
Tell tales of fish who secretly snore.
A starfish yawned, oh what a sight,
While turtles twirled in the moonlight.

With waves styling their wavy hair,
A mermaid juggled seaweed with flair.
Octopus made a fine bouquet,
Threw it to seahorses in ballet.

A walrus in a top hat appeared,
He wobbled and danced, while all cheering cheered.
With a wink, he said, "Join the fiesta!"
A chorus of crabs shouted, "Siesta!"

Oh, serene songs of shells and foam,
Turn every beach into a home.
Where laughter echoes above the waves,
Comedic tales of aquatic braves.

Glide of the Gentle Wave

The gentle waves whisper a tune,
While barnacles play on spoons.
A slippery eel wears a sun hat,
As seagulls shout, "Is that a cat?"

The fish in line for a feathered pie,
Flick their tails and loudly cry.
A stingray slides in a fancy dress,
Making the crowd laugh, oh what a mess!

A school of minnows holds a parade,
While a crab kicks off his clumsy charade.
With bubbles popping all around,
A clownfish giggles, "Is this profound?"

So glide, sweet wave, with rhythmic sway,
In a world where sea creatures play.
With chuckles shared from shore to shore,
In the aqua laughter we all adore.

Beneath the Starlit Waves

Beneath the waves where night owls cheer,
An otter sneaks, "What's that over here?"
With twinkling stars on the ocean floor,
A clam jokes, "Why do fishes snore?"

A surfboard floats, it's way too bright,
Caught in the seaweed, it's quite a sight.
A fish on a skateboard zooms by fast,
Making the turtles laugh till they gasp!

Jellyfish lanterns bloom like a dream,
Painting the scene with a silvery gleam.
A whale sings low, a comical tune,
Echoing laughter under the moon.

So let the waves tickle your toes,
Join the fun where the tide ebbs and flows.
Beneath the stars, let silliness thrive,
In the buoyant world, we come alive!

Siren's Serenade at Twilight

Bubbles rise with every note,
A fishy choir sings afloat.
Octopuses dance with flair,
Seaweed sways without a care.

The crabs tap toes on sandy floor,
While starfish laugh, never a bore.
Clams clap shells in time so neat,
As dolphins join with flips and feats.

Fiddler crabs with tiny props,
Put on shows that never stop.
The ocean giggles through the night,
As waves lap shores with sheer delight.

Then comes a shark, but don't you fret,
He hums along, no need to sweat.
With each refrain, the tides agree,
In the deep, life's just a spree.

Beneath the Waves of Dreams

In coral beds, the jelly winks,
A playful otter cunningly blinks.
Seahorses prance in their fancy hats,
While clowns of the sea prance with spats.

A whale's loud laugh shakes sandy ground,
Echoes bubble, a giddy sound.
Surfers ride on a turtle's back,
As fishes flit in a wiggly pack.

Giggles from a hidden reef,
A dance of bubbles, beyond belief.
Shrimp tap-dance, a vibrant spree,
Spreading joy in the vast deep sea.

With every splash, a tale unfolds,
In this world, magic never gets old.
So close your eyes, drift away with me,
Where dreams are deep, and laughter's free.

Tides of Enchantment

The dolphins giggle, leaping high,
While sea carrots sail and fly.
Mollusks squabble for the best seat,
In an underwater, quirky retreat.

Tides twist tales of finned delights,
Mermaids giggle on starry nights.
With a caper and splash, they tease the squids,
As jellybeans are tossed by kids.

Waves whisper jokes, tickling the shore,
As octopuses prance, begging for more.
A crab tells tales of lost treasures,
Joking about his life's little pleasures.

The sea anemone waves in glee,
In a swirling dance, wild and free.
With each passing tide, a laugh is found,
In this ocean, joy knows no bounds.

Coral Chorus of the Deep

At dusk the coral starts to hum,
Bubbles burble, oh what fun!
Clownfish chuckle in their home,
While sea turtles twirl and roam.

The seahorse struts in a sparkling gown,
While snails slide by with a sleepy frown.
Starfish cheer as they do a jig,
Even the anemones join in big!

An otter juggles with shells galore,
While sea cucumbers ask for more.
Oysters giggle as they sing out loud,
Their sassy tones drawing quite a crowd.

The tide rolls in, the laughter swells,
With every wave, a story tells.
In the depths, where grins abound,
The ocean's chorus is forever found.

Gentle Ripples of Respite

In waters where the fish do dance,
A finned fellow sings a chance.
With bubbles blown and laughter high,
He tickles turtles passing by.

The crabs all clap, a splashing show,
As seaweed sways, in rhythm, flow.
A little octopus out of tune,
Joins in the fun and hums a tune.

The starfish giggle, the jelly leap,
As sea cucumbers quietly creep.
Whispers of shells share silly sights,
In ocean beds, through starry nights.

So drift away on a seafoam dream,
Let laughter spill, like a bubbly stream.
With fishy friends, you can't go wrong,
In playful waves, we all belong.

Deep Blue Dreams and Secrets

With scales that shimmer, tales unfold,
The fishes whisper secrets bold.
A clownfish wearing polka dots,
Tells jokes that leave the sea in knots.

A whale with tones of silly song,
Swings to the rhythm where we belong.
The seaweed giggles, sways with glee,
As dolphins jest, 'Join in the spree!'

Bubbles bob higher, there's much to see,
As deep as the ocean, wild and free.
A seahorse grins, with a nifty spin,
In this ocean of fun, let joy begin!

So close your eyes and breathe in deep,
These ocean secrets are ours to keep.
With laughter rolling along the tide,
In waters wide, where giggles hide.

Mermaid's Restful Rhapsody

A mermaid strums a coral harp,
With melodies bright, they twirl and warp.
She sings to snails, all in a row,
As seagulls chuckle, put on a show.

The shrimp in tuxes, so dapper, so neat,
Dance on the sand with wiggly feet.
They sneak in a twirl, and then a dip,
Creating a splash—what a funny trip!

A crab tries to waltz but trips on sand,
While fishes cheer, they all take a stand.
With every note, the sea ignites,
In rhythmic giggles, the tides unite.

So gather 'round, let giggles soar,
In this playful realm, we'll laugh a score.
With each soft lull, in waves so free,
Our silly song will always be!

Tidepool Tales at Dusk

As sunlight fades, the tidepools shimmer,
Where crabs tell jokes with a cheeky glimmer.
A starfish, wise, sits propped on a rock,
While tiny seashells dance about in a flock.

Anemones sway, in ticklish delight,
As fish spin tales that make day turn to night.
Prawns put on masks, as if in a play,
While seagulls squawk, 'This is the way!'

A slippery eel joins in the fun,
With belly laughs that never shun.
The moon peeks down, casting a grin,
As tidepool giggles begin to spin.

So sit by the shore, let the stories swirl,
With joyous tides as the ocean twirls.
In silly whispers, secrets are kept,
In cheerful waters, where all have leapt.

Ocean's Whispered Serenade

In the depths where fish do dance,
A clam sings songs, a curious chance.
A seahorse twirls, a goofy jest,
While jellyfish jiggle, giving their best.

Starfish giggle as they bop,
A sand dollar joins for a flip-flop.
With seaweed swaying, all is well,
Under moonlit waves, they jingle and tell.

Crabs tickle toes of passing fish,
In bubble parties, they all squish.
Grouper grins with a wink, oh dear,
While sea cucumbers roll with cheer.

So rest your fins in the salty sea,
With shells of laughter, let it be.
Dream of tides that twist and twirl,
As ocean's giggles begin to swirl.

Underwater Dreams and Twilight Tides

In the twilight where fishes play,
A dolphin jests, "Come dance my way!"
With flippers flailing, laughter's gleam,
Bubbles burst in a giggly stream.

Angelfish prance, they take the lead,
A clam commands with a silly speed.
Shrimp do the cha-cha, oh what a sight,
While octopuses juggle, oh-so light.

Starry rays under the moon's bright glow,
Seahorses wink, putting on a show.
Anemones sway, tickling tails,
As laughter echoes through underwater trails.

Catch a wave of their joyful spree,
Join the frolic, swim wild and free.
With shimmering scales, let dreams abide,
In the depths of the ocean, where fun's the guide.

Sonnet of the Shimmering Waves

Under waves where the funny fish glide,
A grouchy puffer, grumpy with glee.
He blows up wide, but can't hide inside,
While minnows giggle, they're light as can be.

A silvery shark with a grin so wide,
Wiggly worm dances, flopping with pride.
The lobsters snap, "Oh, come join the ride!"
With kelp swinging slow, they're never denied.

A joyful whale hums with bubbles to spare,
Who tickles a turtle; it's quite the affair!
Look! Clownfish clowning without a care,
In this merry riptide, there's laughter to share.

So 'neath the waves, let your worries stray,
With shimmering friends, come join the play!

Coral Cradle's Sweet Refrain

In the coral cradle where giggles abound,
A tiny fish whispers, "Don't be profound."
With clownfish prancing, and laughter they gain,
The mollusk chuckles, "What do you sustain?"

Under the surf where the jellyfish float,
A sea turtle dances, stylish and remote.
He accidentally glides right over a snail,
Who spins in circles, leaving a trail.

The anglerfish winks, quite a funny sight,
"Join me for dinner, it's love at first bite!"
But all the fine fish, they simply swim past,
To meet in the current, their giggles amassed.

So rest easy now in this watery space,
With whispers and laughter, feel the warm embrace.
In the cradle of coral, let dreams weave and play,
For the sea sings a tune to brighten the day.

Song of the Midnight Current

Under the waves, where fish like to prance,
A crab joined the dance, in a clumsy romance.
The starfish chuckled, with arms wide in glee,
As the octopus played on his wobbly knee.

Bubbles were bursting, a watery show,
With seaweed confetti, tossed to and fro.
The jellyfish giggled, a glowing parade,
While the seahorse swayed in his tiny charade.

Turtles were twirling, in shells made of gold,
And dolphins jumped high, with stories retold.
In the deep blue, where laughter is bright,
They sang through the currents, all through the night.

Dreaming with Sea Glass Eyes

In dreams of the ocean, where time gently bends,
A clam flips a pancake with all of his friends.
The squids serve up snacks on their flappy old fins,
As the lobster hums tunes that never begin.

The clowns of the reef don their fanciest hats,
And take silly turns, dancing like acrobats.
With bubbles for laughs and corals for cheer,
The fishy fast friends lost all sense of fear.

They giggle and wiggle, in tidal delight,
Sharing mishaps of diving, under moonlight.
With sea glass eyes twinkling, they drift off to dreams,
Where laughter is endless, or so it seems.

Dunes of Dreamy Dusk

On sandy horizons where tides softly play,
The seagulls joke loudly, in a feathery way.
The crabs build their castles, with moats made of foam,
And the flounders all sigh, "Oh, we love our home!"

With whispers of wind, a tickle and tease,
The shells share their gossip, in sunglasses and breeze.
All the oceanic sprites, with mischief in mind,
Sneak snacks from the picnic, and leave laughter behind.

As dusk settles in, the waves start to hum,
The air is abuzz, oh, what a big drum!
Shellfish and seahorses, in shimmery duds,
Dance under the stars, in their very own floods.

Neptune's Nighttime Refrain

When night falls upon the great briny deep,
Neptune rolls out, ready for some leap.
With his trident in one hand, a flick of his wrist,
He summons up sea creatures, all pals on his list.

The anglerfish giggles, with her lamp shining bright,
As they gather for stories and a big water fight.
From clownfish to flounder, they share their best tales,
Of treasure-filled chests and adventurous sails.

With laughter like bubbles, and splashy replays,
They tickle the seaweed, for silly displays.
Together they twinkle, in Neptune's grand show,
A symphony of giggles, where dark waters flow.

www.ingramcontent.com/pod-product-compliance
Lightning Source LLC
Chambersburg PA
CBHW060127230426
43661CB00003B/361